DATE DUE

TOP TEN
COUNTRIES
OF RECENT
IMMIGRANTS

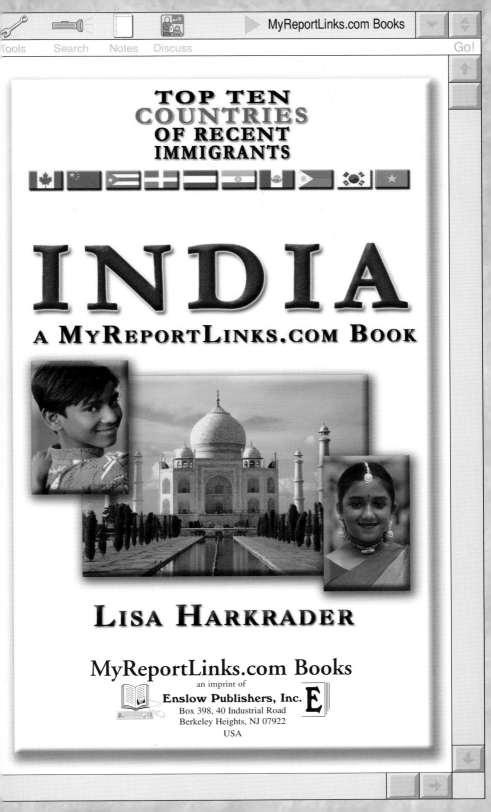

INDIA
A MYREPORTLINKS.COM BOOK

LISA HARKRADER

MyReportLinks.com Books
an imprint of
Enslow Publishers, Inc. E
Box 398, 40 Industrial Road
Berkeley Heights, NJ 07922
USA

MyReportLinks.com Books, an imprint of Enslow Publishers, Inc. MyReportLinks®
is a registered trademark of Enslow Publishers, Inc.

Library of Congress Cataloging-in-Publication Data

Harkrader, Lisa.
  India / Lisa Harkrader.
    v. cm — (Top ten countries of recent immigrants)
Includes bibliographical references and index.
Contents: India : a land of diversity—Land and climate—Culture—
Economy—History—Indian Americans.
  ISBN 0-7660-5180-3
  1. India—Juvenile literature. 2. East Indian Americans—Juvenile
literature. [1. India. 2. East Indian Americans.] I. Title. II. Series.

  DS407.H265 2004
  954—dc22
                                    2003015123

Printed in the United States of America

10 9 8 7 6 5 4 3 2 1

To Our Readers:
Through the purchase of this book, you and your library gain access to the Report Links that specifically back up this book.
The Publisher will provide access to the Report Links that back up this book and will keep these Report Links up to date on **www.myreportlinks.com** for three years from the book's first publication date.
We have done our best to make sure all Internet addresses in this book were active and appropriate when we went to press. However, the author and the Publisher have no control over, and assume no liability for, the material available on those Internet sites or on other Web sites they may link to.
The usage of the MyReportLinks.com Books Web site is subject to the terms and conditions stated on the Usage Policy Statement on **www.myreportlinks.com**.
A password may be required to access the Report Links that back up this book. The password is found on the bottom of page 4 of this book.
Any comments or suggestions can be sent by e-mail to comments@myreportlinks.com or to the address on the back cover.

Photo Credits: © Corel Corporation, pp. 1, 9 (flag), 11, 20, 23, 28, 30, 37; AP/Wide World Photos, pp. 41, 43; Artville, p. 3; Bengal-Tigers.org, p. 19; CNN.com, p. 24; Enslow Publishers, Inc., p. 16; Harvard-Smithsonian Center for Astrophysics, p. 44; Manas, pp. 26, 35; MyReportLinks.com Books, p. 4, back cover; PBS, p. 33; TIME.com, p. 13.

Cover Photo: © Corel Corporation, flags, Taj Mahal; boy, Painet Stock Photos; girl, Photos.com.

Tools   Search   Notes   Discuss   Go!

Contents

INDIA

MyReportLinks.com Books
Great Books, Great Links, Great for Research!

The Report Links listed on the following four pages can save you hours of research time by **instantly** bringing you to the best Web sites relating to your report topic.

How to Use MyReportLinks.com

1 Got a Report to do?

2 Check out a MyReportLinks.com Book at the Library.

3 Read the Book.

4 Go to www.myreportlinks.com for Quick, Safe, and Up-to-Date Links!

5 Internet Report Links = Great Information.

6 Write Your Report. Impress Your Teacher.

MAX LYNX

The pre-evaluated Web sites are your links to source documents, photographs, illustrations, and maps. They also provide links to dozens—even hundreds—of Web sites about your report subject.

MyReportLinks.com Books and the MyReportLinks.com Web site save you time and make report writing easier than ever!

Please see "To Our Readers" on the copyright page for important information about this book, the MyReportLinks.com Web site, and the Report Links that back up this book. Please enter **IIN1080** if asked for a password.

Report Links

The Internet sites described below can be accessed at
http://www.myreportlinks.com

The *World Factbook*: India
*EDITOR'S CHOICE

From the CIA *World Factbook*, you can find out information on India. Geography, people, government, and economy are some of the covered topics.

Go Places: India
*EDITOR'S CHOICE

This *Time Magazine for Kids* site offers a glimpse into Indian life. It includes a sightseeing guide, a time line, a quiz, and more.

Mohandas Gandhi
*EDITOR'S CHOICE

Mohandas Gandhi led nonviolent protests against the British rule of India. At this site from *Time* magazine, you can read about his life and influence in Indian and world history.

India and the Himalayas
*EDITOR'S CHOICE

India's history, religious practices, culture, geography, and more are explored in this interesting Web site.

India and Pakistan: 50 Years of Independence
*EDITOR'S CHOICE

This site contains a wealth of information on the history of India and Pakistan since 1947, when India became an independent nation and Pakistan was created from it.

Taj Mahal
*EDITOR'S CHOICE

The Taj Mahal is one of India's most famous and beautiful architectural works. This site includes information about its history and structure as well as several images.

The Internet sites described below can be accessed at http://www.myreportlinks.com

▶**The Beginning of the British Raj**
This time line, from 1661 to 1760, documents the beginnings of British rule in India, the period known as the Raj.

▶**Bengal Tigers**
Learn about the Bengal tiger, or Indian tiger, which is native to India and Bangladesh.

▶**A Brief History of Indian Immigration to America**
This site contains a look at the history of Indian immigration to the United States and examines the effect on those immigrants of life in America.

▶**Chandra X-Ray Observatory Center: Subrahmanyan Chandrasekl**
Subrahmanyan Chandrasekhar was a Nobel Prize-winning astrophysicist who emigrated from India to the United States in 1937. Read about his life and the NASA observatory named for him.

▶**The Dalai Lama: Spiritual Leader in Exile**
This CNN site profiles the Dalai Lama, the Buddhist leader of the Tibetan people, who lives in exile in India. Included are recent news reports and videos.

▶**Delhi-India: History and Times**
This site provides information about India's capital city region, including its culture, history, people, and architecture.

▶**Embassy of India in Washington, D.C.**
This site connects you with the Indian Embassy to the United States, which is headquartered in Washington D.C. It contains links to Indian current events, government, and cultural information.

▶**Fact Sheets: Indian Peafowl**
The national bird of India is the peacock. The Smithsonian's National Zoo site provides information on this beautiful bird, including its habitat, diet, and more.

Report Links

The Internet sites described below can be accessed at
http://www.myreportlinks.com

The Film Industry in India
India produces more films per year than any other country in the world.
Learn about the history of its bustling movie industry.

Greeting India
At this site, explore India's unique culture, history, geography, and more.

The Himalayas
This U.S. government site provides detailed information about the Himalayas,
which form part of India's northern border.

Hinduism
This BBC site offers an introduction to India's most widely practiced religion,
and one of the world's oldest religions, Hinduism.

India/Pakistan: A History of Conflict
This site includes information about the tensions and conflicts between India
and Pakistan, which have existed for more than fifty years. Includes a time
line, maps of their territories, and links to related topics.

Indian Festivals
The history and cultural origins of India's unique festivals and holidays are
examined in this site.

India Image
This site offers links to information on the Web provided by the Indian
government. Learn about India's national flag, flower, anthem, and more.

Indian Instruments
This site takes a look at some of the musical instruments that have been part
of India's culture throughout its long history.

Report Links

The Internet sites described below can be accessed at http://www.myreportlinks.com

▶**Indian Museum, Kolkata**

The official Web site of the Indian Museum in Kolkata (Calcutta) provides a great look at Indian art and culture. You can view individual parts of the collection as well as learn about the museum in general.

▶**Indian Music**

The history of Indian music, from its origins to modern times, is explored in this site.

▶**Indian Mythology**

This site takes a look at the history surrounding many of the myths, legends, and beliefs that form the foundation of Indian mythology.

▶**Manas: India and its Neighbors**

This comprehensive site offers an in-depth look at many aspects of India—its history, culture, geography, and more.

▶**Ravi Shankar**

Ravi Shankar is one of the most widely recognized musicians in the world. Learn about the legendary sitar player at this site, which includes pictures, a biography, and information about Indian music.

▶**Soul of India: Time Line**

This time line of Indian history focuses on Hindu and Muslim relations over a span of several thousand years and presents information on ancient empires, British India, and Pakistan.

▶***USA Today*.com: Indians the Fastest-Growing Asian Group**

This *USA Today* news article provides information about the growing Indian population in the United States in relation to other Asian populations.

▶**WWF-India: Endangered Species**

This World Wildlife Fund site describes several endangered species that are native to India, including the Asiatic lion and the red panda.

India Facts

Official Name
Republic of India

Capital
New Delhi

Population
1,049,700,118
(July 2003 estimate)[1]

Area
1,269,438 square miles
(3,287,590 square kilometers)[2]

Highest Point
Kanchenjunga, 28,208 feet
(8,598 meters)

Lowest Point
Sea level

Location
South central Asia

Type of Government
Federal republic

Head of State
President

Head of Government
Prime minister

Monetary Unit
Rupee

Official Languages
According to India's constitution, there are seventeen official languages, with Hindi the national language.

National Anthem
"Jana Gana Mana" ("Thou Art the Ruler of All Minds")

National Song
"Vande Mataram" ("I Bow to Thee, Mother")

National Flower
Lotus

National Tree
Banyan

National Fruit
Mango

National Bird
Peacock

National Animal
Bengal tiger

Flag
India's flag, which was adopted on July 22, 1947, features three horizontal bands of saffron, white, and dark green. The saffron, the color of the Hindu faith, represents courage, sacrifice, patriotism, and renunciation. The green, the color of Islam, represents faith, fertility, and the land. The white symbolizes a hope for peace and unity. In the center of the white band is the Ashoka Chakra, a blue wheel with 24 spokes, which represents India's continual progress and the importance of justice in the life of the nation.

India: A Land of Diversity

India, in southern Asia, is the seventh largest country in the world in area and the second largest in population, after China. Over a billion people live in India.

For thousands of years, travelers, adventurers, and invaders settled in the land that is now India. These people brought their own religions, customs, and languages. Today, India is a rich mixture of diverse cultures. Hindi is the national language, but India has seventeen official languages, and English is the most important language for national, political, and commercial communication. In fact, India has the second-largest English-speaking population in the world, after the United States. There are at least thirty-five languages spoken by more than a million people in India, and there are about 22,000 dialects within those languages.

In India, one can find the most advanced modern technology and the most ancient farming methods. India is also home to jewel-encrusted palaces as well as thatched-roof mud huts. Some Indians wear modern western fashions and others wear traditional draped saris and loose pants known as pyjamas. In India are some of the hottest places on earth and some of the coldest; some of the wettest hillsides and some of the driest deserts; some of the tallest mountains and some of the flattest plains—all within the same country. And India is home to one of the most famous and beautiful architectural structures in the world—the Taj Mahal.

The Taj Mahal

A shimmering white marble tomb or mausoleum towers above the Yamuna River in the northern Indian city of Agra. This domed mausoleum is the Taj Mahal.

Shah Jahan, the Mughal emperor who ruled northern India from 1628 to 1658, built the Taj Mahal. Shah Jahan had several wives, but Mumtaz Mahal was his most beloved. In 1631, Mumtaz Mahal died while giving birth to her fourteenth child. Shah Jahan was heartbroken. He wanted to show how much he had loved her. The Mughals prized grand architecture, so Shah Jahan decided to honor his wife by creating the most magnificent tomb the world had ever seen.

Shah Jahan hired artisans from as far away as Turkey. He imported precious gems from China, Russia, Egypt, Afghanistan, and Tibet. He sent a thousand elephants

▲ The Taj Mahal symbolizes the beauty and grace of India.

to haul blue-veined white marble from Makrana, a city nearly two hundred miles away. Twenty thousand workers labored for twenty-two years. Finally, in 1643, the Taj Mahal was finished.

In 1658, one of his sons captured Shah Jahan and declared himself emperor. Shah Jahan spent the next eight years in prison. He died in 1666. Shah Jahan was buried beside his beloved wife in the Taj Mahal.

▶ Great Soul

India was also the birthplace of one of the most influential political and spiritual leaders of the twentieth century—Mohandas Karamchand Gandhi. Gandhi was born in Porbandar in western India in 1869. He attended law school in London. In 1893, he moved to South Africa, where he began practicing law for an Indian company. In South Africa, Indian immigrants did not have many rights. Laws banned Indians from voting or owning land, and the South African government did not recognize Indian marriages.

Gandhi experienced the injustice firsthand. When he arrived in South Africa, railroad officials would not let him ride in the first-class passenger car of a train, even though he had a first-class ticket, because of his skin color. They forced him off the train, onto the platform. In 1896, white South Africans beat Gandhi simply for trying to get off a ship with his family. Gandhi urged his fellow Indians in South Africa to peacefully refuse to follow unfair laws. He called this peaceful refusal *satyagraha*. Satyagraha combines two Sanskrit words: *satya* (truth and love) and *agraha* (firmness). Gandhi believed that Indians could win equal rights by displaying truth, love, and firmness rather than by using violence.

In 1915, Gandhi returned to India, which was then under British rule. He believed that India should, through the nonviolent ways of satyagraha, work to become an independent nation. Gandhi believed that the two largest religious groups in India, Hindus and Muslims, needed to set aside their differences and work together. He also believed that Hindus known as untouchables, who were members of the lowest caste, or social class, should have the same rights as other Indians. Other Hindus considered untouchables unclean, allowing them to do only the most menial jobs, such as sweeping the streets or emptying bedpans. But Gandhi thought Indians in higher castes should accept untouchables.

Millions of Indians began following Gandhi, whom they called *Mahatma*, which means "Great Soul." His

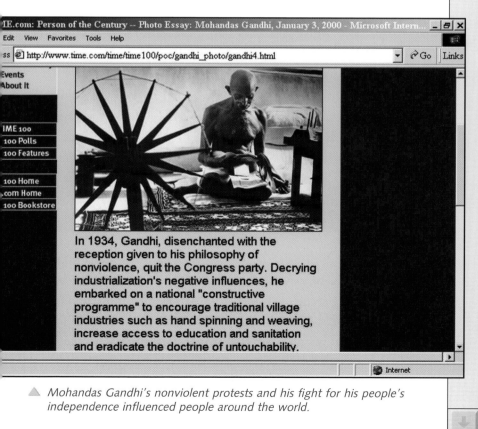

In 1934, Gandhi, disenchanted with the reception given to his philosophy of nonviolence, quit the Congress party. Decrying industrialization's negative influences, he embarked on a national "constructive programme" to encourage traditional village industries such as hand spinning and weaving, increase access to education and sanitation and eradicate the doctrine of untouchability.

▲ Mohandas Gandhi's nonviolent protests and his fight for his people's independence influenced people around the world.

nonviolent protests against British rule led many Indians to quit their jobs in the British government. Others pulled their children out of government schools. They also refused to pay taxes. Gandhi encouraged Indians to spin their own yarn instead of buying British cloth. The spinning wheel soon became a symbol of Indian independence. Gandhi also encouraged Indians to gather sea salt to protest the British salt tax. British officials imprisoned Gandhi several times for his acts of civil disobedience. Finally released in 1944, Gandhi was one of the most important figures in helping India to achieve its independence from Great Britain on August 15, 1947.

He did not live to see his country enjoy its independence for long, however. On January 30, 1948, Gandhi was walking to a prayer meeting. A Hindu fanatic, angry because he believed Gandhi cared too much for Muslims, shot and killed the Great Soul.

Gandhi is still loved and revered in India. Indians call him the "Father of the Nation." His ideas of satyagraha have influenced leaders around the world, including Dr. Martin Luther King, Jr. Dr. King put into practice Gandhi's ideas of nonviolent civil disobedience in his fight for civil rights for African Americans in the United States.

▶ Renaming Towns

When the British ruled India, they gave names to many of the cities. In recent years, the Indian government has begun replacing some of these British names with more traditional Indian names. The city of Bombay is now called Mumbai. Calcutta became Kolkata. Madras became Chennai. But while Mumbai, Kolkata, and Chennai are now the official names, Indians use the old names as often as they use the new names. Most people outside India still use the old names.

Land and Climate

Most of India lies in what is known as the Indian subcontinent, which juts into the Indian Ocean. It joins the rest of Asia only along its northern border. India is bordered by Pakistan, China, Nepal, Tibet, Bhutan, Bangladesh, and Myanmar (formerly known as Burma).

The Lay of the Land

Millions of years ago, the Indian subcontinent was a separate island. When this island crashed into Asia, it shoved the edges of both lands up, creating the Himalayan mountain range.

The snow-capped Himalayas line India's northern border. They are the tallest and the youngest mountains in the world. Mount Everest, the world's highest mountain at 29,035 feet (8,850 meters), lies in the Himalayas between Nepal and Tibet. The tallest peak in India is Kanchenjunga. It soars to 28,208 feet (8,598 meters) and is the third highest mountain in the world.

The Ganges River begins in an ice cave in the Himalayas. The Ganges is one of the most important rivers in India, and Hindus consider it holy. It flows from the mountains and across the wide Gangetic Plain. This lush flatland stretches across India at the base of the Himalayas. The Gangetic Plain is one of the most fertile places in the world. It is also one of the most densely populated. In the rich soil of this region, Indians grow wheat, rice, sugarcane, and other crops on tiny family farms.

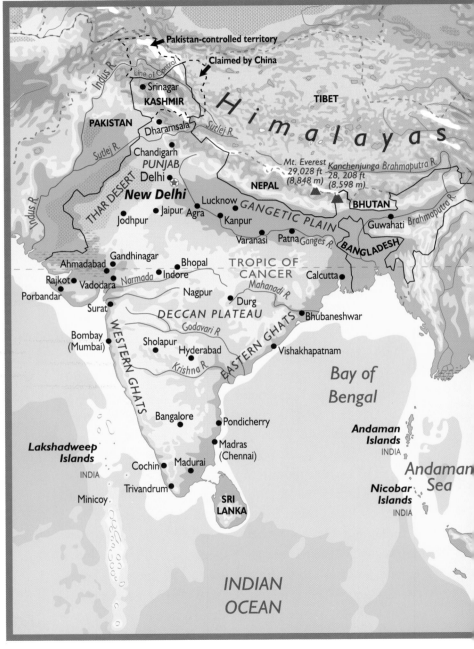

Pakistan-controlled territory
Claimed by China

Indus R.

Line of Control

Srinagar

KASHMIR

TIBET

Himalayas

PAKISTAN

Dharamsala

Sutlej R.

Chandigarh

PUNJAB

Sutlej R.

Delhi

New Delhi

Mt. Everest
29,028 ft
(8,848 m)

Kanchenjunga
28, 208 ft
(8,598 m)

Brahmaputra R.

NEPAL

BHUTAN

THAR DESERT

Jodhpur

Jaipur

Agra

Lucknow

Kanpur

GANGETIC PLAIN

Guwahati

Brahmaputra R.

Indus R.

Varanasi

Patna

Ganges R.

BANGLADESH

Ahmadabad

Gandhinagar

Bhopal

TROPIC OF
CANCER

Calcutta

Rajkot

Vadodara

Narmada

Indore

Porbandar

Nagpur

Mahanadi R.

Surat

Durg

DECCAN PLATEAU

Bhubaneshwar

Bombay
(Mumbai)

Godavari R.

EASTERN GHATS

Sholapur

Hyderabad

Krishna R.

Vishakhapatnam

WESTERN GHATS

Bangalore

Pondicherry

Bay of
Bengal

Andaman
Islands

INDIA

*Lakshadweep
Islands*

Madras
(Chennai)

INDIA

Cochin

Madurai

*Andaman
Sea*

Trivandrum

Minicoy

SRI
LANKA

*Nicobar
Islands*

INDIA

INDIAN
OCEAN

▲ *A map of India.*

South of the Gangetic Plain is the rocky Deccan Plateau. The plateau covers the southern triangular-shaped part of India. In this region lie India's diamond, gold, silver, and copper mines. The area is also rich in iron, coal, beautiful Indian marble, and the red sandstone that Mughal emperors used to build magnificent palaces and forts. Two ranges of wooded hills, the Western Ghats and the Eastern Ghats, border the Deccan Plateau on each side. The two ranges meet at the southern tip of India.

Hot and Cold, Wet and Dry

India has three seasons: winter, summer, and monsoon. But India is such a large country that the climate varies drastically from north to south and east to west.

Winter begins in November and lasts through January. Winter in the Himalayas is long and cold. Snow chokes mountain passes for almost half the year. South of the Himalayas, though, India is a tropical country. In southern India, winter is pleasantly warm.

Summer lasts from February to May. The mountaintops of the Himalayas stay frozen and snow-packed, but the lower slopes and foothills warm up and become comfortably cool. Many Indians spend the summer in the Himalayas to escape the blistering heat of central and southern India.

Monsoons storm across India from June to August. Monsoons are winds that blow in from the Indian Ocean and dump heavy rains across the land. Indian farmers rely on the rain to grow their crops. When the monsoon does not bring enough rain, the country faces drought. But monsoon season can be a dangerous time. Floods surge through cities and villages. Cyclones blast India's eastern coast.

Cherrapunji, a small town in northeastern India, holds the world record for most rainfall in a year. From August

1860 to July 1861, over 1,041 inches (2,646 centimeters) of rain fell in Cherrapunji.[1] The nearby town of Mawsynram holds the world record for average rainfall. An average of 467 inches of rain falls on Mawsynram per year.[2]

The least rain falls on the Thar Desert, a scorching area of shifting sand dunes that sweeps across northwestern India into Pakistan. This region receives less than eight inches (twenty centimeters) of rain each year.

▶ Exotic and Endangered

The lotus, India's national flower, grows in ponds and rivers. The blossom of the lotus floats above the water. Palm trees and tropical fruit trees, such as mango (the national fruit of India), banana, and papaya, also flourish in India's warm climate. The banyan is India's national tree. Indians consider it sacred. The banyan sends roots down from its branches to form new trunks. In this way, a single banyan tree can spread to a width of forty feet.

Teak, rosewood, and sandalwood trees cover the Western Ghats. Teak and rosewood have very hard wood that makes long-lasting furniture. Sandalwood grows on the roots and stems of other plants and trees. The oil from sandalwood is used as an ingredient in perfumes, soaps, and natural medicine.

India is home to a wide variety of animals. The peacock, India's national bird, lives in jungles and forests across India. Male peacocks are famous for their mating dance. The male fans his brilliant green and gold tail feathers and struts for the female, called a peahen.

India is the one of the few countries in the world where both lions and tigers live in the wild. The lions found in India, Asiatic lions, are smaller than the lions found in Africa. The males have shorter manes. These lions once roamed wild from southern Europe to India. Today only two to three hundred Asiatic lions remain. They live in the Gir National Park in western India. Bengal tigers, India's national animal, once ranged throughout the Indian subcontinent. In the early 1900s, about forty thousand tigers lived in India. Now fewer than four thousand are left. But in the last decade, conservation efforts to preserve the species, including 25 reserves, have helped increase the population of Bengal tigers.

Asian elephants live in the forests of India. Asian elephants are sometimes called Indian elephants. They are smaller than African elephants. They have smaller ears, and their skin is less wrinkled. Indian rhinoceroses live in north-western grasslands. These one-horned rhinos have folds of

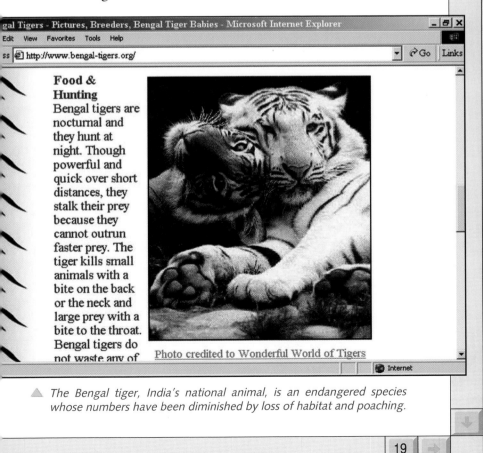

gal Tigers - Pictures, Breeders, Bengal Tiger Babies - Microsoft Internet Explorer

Edit   View   Favorites   Tools   Help

ss   http://www.bengal-tigers.org/   Go   Links

Food & Hunting
Bengal tigers are nocturnal and they hunt at night. Though powerful and quick over short distances, they stalk their prey because they cannot outrun faster prey. The tiger kills small animals with a bite on the back or the neck and large prey with a bite to the throat. Bengal tigers do not waste any of

Photo credited to Wonderful World of Tigers

Internet

The Bengal tiger, India's national animal, is an endangered species whose numbers have been diminished by loss of habitat and poaching.

skin that look like suits of armor. Snow leopards live high in the rugged Himalayas. They have thick, yellowish-white fur with dark spots. Their fur helps protect and hide them in the snow-covered mountains. Elephants, rhinos, and snow leopards are all endangered species.

Many of these animals are dying out because their habitats have disappeared. India's forests have been cleared for farming, mining, dams, housing, and fuel. Poachers kill elephants for their ivory tusks, and tigers, lions, and snow leopards for their skins. They kill rhinos for their horns, which some people use as medicine. India has passed laws to protect these animals, and many of India's endangered species now live in nature reserves.

▲ The peacock is India's national bird.

Culture

India is a whirl of activity and color. Colorful hand-painted billboards advertise Indian movies. Bright banners, flags, and kites fly during Indian festivals. Indians wear clothing of vibrant orange, red, pink, yellow, blue, and purple.

Traditionally, Indians feel a strong duty toward their family. Grandparents, parents, children, aunts, and uncles often live together in the same house. Parents usually arrange marriages for their children. Children often take care of their parents and grandparents when they become older.

Language

Although the national language of India is Hindi, the government recognizes seventeen official languages, including Assamese, Bengali, Gujarati, Hindi, Kannada, Kashmiri, Malayalam, Marathi, Oriya, Punjabi, Sanskrit, Sindhi, Tamil, Telugu, and Urdu.[1] There are more than 35 languages and 22,000 dialects spoken in India. More than 70 million Indians are Adivasis, tribal people who live in the hills and forests of India. Many tribal groups speak their own local languages.

Since Great Britain ruled India for two centuries, many Indians speak English. They often use English to communicate with people from other regions who speak a different Indian language. Indian schools teach Hindi and English along with the local language.

Religion

Many faiths are practiced in India. Religion is a basic part of the lives of most Indians. It determines how they dress, how they behave, and what they eat.

Over 80 percent of Indians practice Hinduism, a religion that developed in India about four thousand years ago. Hindus believe in many gods and goddesses. They also believe in reincarnation. They believe that if a person does good deeds during his life, after he dies he will be reborn into a better life. If he does bad deeds, he will come back as a lower life-form, such as a worm or an insect. Most Hindus are vegetarians. To Hindus, cows are sacred, and Hindus do not eat beef.

Hindus developed a caste system, in which people are treated according to social class or rank. The highest caste is the Brahmans, or priests. Below all the castes are the untouchables, who are considered unclean. Hindus are born into their caste. They cannot rise out of it. The government outlawed the caste system in 1950, but many Hindus still follow it.

About 12 percent of Indians are Muslims. Muslims follow Islam, a religion brought to India during the Mughal Empire, which ruled India from 1526 to 1827, and by other Muslims who invaded the country. Muslims believe there is one god, called Allah. Muslims pray five times a day while facing Mecca, the city in Saudi Arabia where Allah's prophet, Muhammad, was born. A man called a muezzin calls them to prayer. He stands in a tall tower atop a Muslim mosque, or temple. This tower is called minaret.

About 2 percent of Indians are Sikhs. Most Sikhs live in the Punjab in northwestern India. A man named Guru Nanak founded Sikhism in the 1500s. It is a combination of Hinduism and Islam. Sikhs believe in one god, as Muslims do. They also reject the caste system. Like Hindus, Sikhs believe in reincarnation. Sikhs do not smoke or drink. Sikh men do not cut their hair or beards. They usually wear turbans.

About twenty-five hundred years ago, a Hindu prince gave away his wealth and began searching for a more satisfying life. He became known as Buddha. The religion he founded is called Buddhism. Buddhists do not believe in the caste system. They do not pray to gods. Instead, they look within themselves for truth. Although Buddhism began in India and has spread throughout the world, today less than one percent of Indians are Buddhists. Most Indian Buddhists live near the Himalayas. The Dalai Lama, the leader of Tibetan Buddhism, lives in an old British garrison called McLeod Ganj, in Dharamsala, a Himalayan city in northern India. The Dalai Lama moved his headquarters to northern India in 1959 after China seized Tibet.

Statues of Hindu gods and goddesses can be found in both the great palaces and common areas of India.

Jainism began in India at about the same time that Buddhism had its beginnings there. A wealthy Hindu named Mahavira gave away his fortune. He wandered India, searching for a more fulfilling way of life. His beliefs became the foundation of Jainism. Jains believe in reincarnation, but they do not believe in gods or the caste system. They are vegetarians who do not kill animals. Less than one percent of Indians are Jains.

Almost 3 percent of Indians are Christians, who profess belief in the teachings of Jesus Christ and believe the Bible is sacred scripture. According to legend, Saint Thomas, one of Jesus' apostles, came to Kerala, on the western coast of India, in A.D. 52 and is believed to have converted many people to

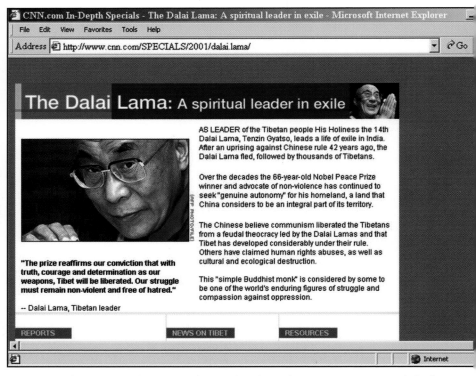

CNN.com In-Depth Specials - The Dalai Lama: A spiritual leader in exile - Microsoft Internet Explorer

File   Edit   View   Favorites   Tools   Help

Address http://www.cnn.com/SPECIALS/2001/dalai.lama/   Go

The Dalai Lama: A spiritual leader in exile

(AFP PHOTO/FILE)

AS LEADER of the Tibetan people His Holiness the 14th Dalai Lama, Tenzin Gyatso, leads a life of exile in India. After an uprising against Chinese rule 42 years ago, the Dalai Lama fled, followed by thousands of Tibetans.

Over the decades the 66-year-old Nobel Peace Prize winner and advocate of non-violence has continued to seek "genuine autonomy" for his homeland, a land that China considers to be an integral part of its territory.

The Chinese believe communism liberated the Tibetans from a feudal theocracy led by the Dalai Lamas and that Tibet has developed considerably under their rule. Others have claimed human rights abuses, as well as cultural and ecological destruction.

"The prize reaffirms our conviction that with truth, courage and determination as our weapons, Tibet will be liberated. Our struggle must remain non-violent and free of hatred."

-- Dalai Lama, Tibetan leader

This "simple Buddhist monk" is considered by some to be one of the world's enduring figures of struggle and compassion against oppression.

REPORTS   NEWS ON TIBET   RESOURCES

Internet

△ Although living in exile in India, the Dalai Lama continues to fight for Tibet's liberation from China.

Christianity. In the 1500s, the Portuguese settled Goa, a city in Kerala. The Portuguese were Roman Catholic, and today many Indians in Goa are Catholic. For centuries, Christian missionaries from European countries converted many Indians to their faith. Mother Teresa, a Catholic nun, established the Missionaries of Charity in Kolkata (Calcutta). For nearly fifty years, Mother Teresa helped the poor and sick who lived on the streets of that city. She was awarded the 1979 Nobel Peace Prize for her work among those people and was beatified by Pope John Paul II in October 2003.

Some Indians practice Zoroastrianism, a religion founded in Persia in the sixth century B.C. by the prophet Zoroaster. Zoroastrians worship a supreme god named Ahura Mazda who asks for their good deeds in order to battle an evil spirit named Ahriman. Indian Zoroastrians are called Parsis. Most Parsis live in Mumbai (Bombay).

Festivals

Indian life is filled with holidays and holy days, celebrated throughout the year with hundreds of festivals. Some are small village festivals, while others are huge national festivals. Some of the festivals celebrate religious events. Some celebrate national holidays, such as Republic Day, Independence Day, and Mahatma Gandhi's birthday. Some celebrate seasons, harvests, or animals such as camels and elephants. The festivals are colorful and lively, filled with music, dancing, and parades.

Many festivals honor the Hindu god Rama. During the ten days of the festival of Dussehra, Hindus perform plays to celebrate Rama's triumph over the demon-king Ravana. Hindus celebrate Diwali for five days. This festival is also called the Festival of Lights. Diwali signifies different things in different parts of the country, but it is

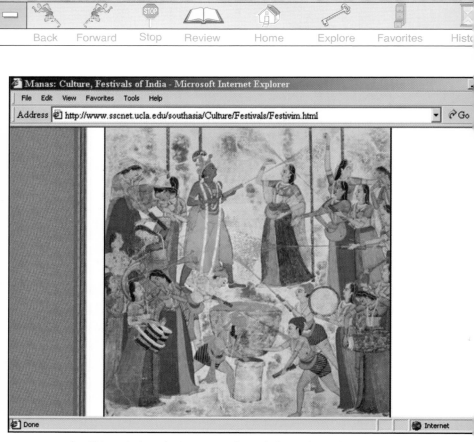

File   Edit   View   Favorites   Tools   Help

Address http://www.sscnet.ucla.edu/southasia/Culture/Festivals/Festivim.html   Go

Done   Internet

This painting depicts an early Holi festival in which the Hindu god Krishna is celebrated.

always a celebration of renewal and hope. Hindus line ledges and balconies with lights or clay lamps. They shoot off fireworks and give each other boxes of candy.

Holi is a Hindu festival that celebrates the beginning of spring. During the festival, Hindus dance, sing, and light bonfires. They throw colored water and paint on each other. The water and paint represent the colors of spring.

Makar Sankranti, or the Kite Festival, takes place on January 14. During Makar Sankranti, Indians fly brightly colored kites. They compete in kite contests. People in southern India celebrate the rice harvest with a festival called Pongal. They decorate cows and feed them sweetened rice, hoping for a good harvest the next year.

Economy

Nearly 60 percent of India's land is farmland, and two thirds of Indian workers are farmers. Most farms are no bigger than one or two acres, and many farmers still use traditional methods to work their land. They plant and harvest crops by hand. Cattle or water buffalo pull their plows. In the 1960s, however, a "green revolution" ushered in more modern agricultural methods, and India's agricultural production benefited.

Wheat and other grains grow in the fertile plains of northern India. Rice grows in flooded paddies in southern and eastern India. Rubber trees grow in the hot southern tip of the country. Indian farmers also grow sugarcane, cotton, coffee, and legumes such as chickpeas. India is a leading producer of bananas, mangoes, coconuts, cashews, and milk.

Grocery stores around the world sell teas with exotic-sounding names like Darjeeling and Assam. These teas are named for places in northeastern India. India is famous for its tea. It grows more tea than any other country in the world. Tea plantations cover the lush, wet hillsides of northeastern India. Tea also grows in the mountains at the southern tip of India.

Monsoons give India the perfect climate to grow certain crops. The monsoon rains flood rice paddies and keep tea plantations moist and humid. But monsoons can sometimes be unreliable. Too much rain brings floods. Too little rain brings drought. Both floods and drought can

▲ *The Indus Valley, in northwestern India, was the birthplace of Indian civilization. Here, the region is pictured at harvest season.*

cause crops to fail. The Indian government keeps large stores of grain for emergencies. When bad weather ruins the year's crop, the grain reserves keep India's people from starving.

▶ The Spice Trade

Monsoons create the perfect climate for growing pepper and other spices. Spices have been important to the Indian economy since its beginnings. For centuries, Arab merchants brought spices from India to western countries. They traveled by camel caravan over thousands of miles of rugged terrain. The Romans discovered sea routes to India in the first century A.D.

For centuries, spices were more valuable than gold. People used spices not only to flavor food, but also to preserve food, mask the rancid taste of spoiled food, and cover bad odors. They used spices in perfumes and medicines. By the sixteenth century, European countries began looking for cheaper ways to obtain spices. England, France, Portugal, Spain, and Holland tried to find their own routes to India. These countries established trading companies in spice-growing regions. They fought wars over the Indian spice trade.

Today, spices are not as valuable as gold, but they are still important crops in India and important exports. Indian black pepper is the finest pepper in the world. India also grows cardamom, cinnamon, cloves, cumin, ginger, nutmeg, turmeric, and vanilla.

Ancient Arts and Advanced Technology

India has been home to the finest silk, cotton, and wool clothing for centuries. India is famous for its richly dyed and decorated fabrics. That tradition continues, and today India is one of the world's top producers of fabric and clothing. Some of these textiles are made in factories. Some are made by hand.

Many of the handmade fabrics, as well as other crafts, come from India's villages. Village artists create about half of all products in India. Villagers in Kashmir weave elegant shawls from goat fleece and the soft under hairs of Tibetan antelopes. Jewelers in Jaipur create fine jewelry and ornaments from gems and enameled metal. In other villages, folk artists make pottery, silverware, paintings, hand-carved wooden boxes and toys, hand-stitched leather shoes and bags, and hand-knotted carpets. Many of these artists learned their crafts from their parents and have handed them down to their children.

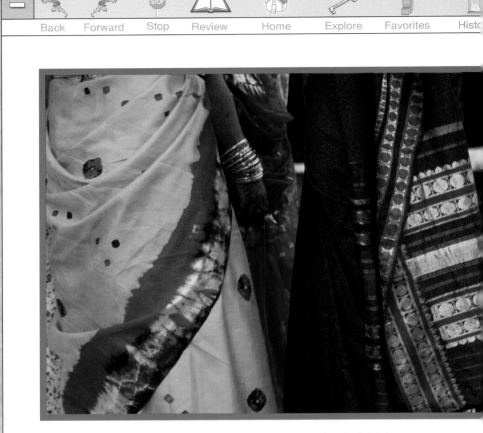

▲ *India has long been known for its rich and colorful fabrics, as seen here in the traditional saris worn by Indian women.*

While some Indians earn their living working at ancient crafts, other Indians work in India's growing high-tech industry. The Indian Institute of Technology (IIT) is one of the finest engineering and technology schools in the world. Technology companies around the world compete to hire IIT graduates. Other graduates have started their own technology companies in India and other countries.[1] India is now a world leader in software development.

▶ Hooray for Bollywood

Movies are extremely popular in India. Indian filmmakers produce between eight hundred and nine hundred films each year. In fact, more movies are made in India than in any other country in the world, including the United States.[2]

The heart of India's movie industry is Mumbai. Indians call this movie-making center Bollywood, after America's Hollywood. Bollywood movies are colorful, like India itself. The typical Bollywood film is a romantic musical. It is usually set in an exotic place and involves lots of action and glamour. Many Indian movies are in Hindi, but other movies are made in English, Tamil, Bengali, and other languages. One of the most influential moviemakers of the twentieth century was the Indian Satyajit Ray, whose movies were mostly in Bengali.

Wealth and Poverty

Since the 1990s, India's booming technology industry has created many new Indian millionaires. It has also expanded the middle class. But about 35 percent of Indians still live in poverty. The poorest Indians live on patches of sidewalk in cities such as Mumbai and Kolkata. Many of these homeless people are farmers who came to the city to find jobs. They left their villages because floods, droughts, famine, and other conditions forced them to seek better opportunities in larger cities.

History

The first civilizations rose up on the Indian subcontinent hundreds of thousands of years ago. These ancient people began farming and settling in villages. By 2500 B.C., a great civilization prospered around the Indus River in Pakistan and northwestern India. The Indus Valley people lived in well-planned cities. They built water and sewage systems. They traded with civilizations as far away as Mesopotamia. Their religion contained the earliest elements of Hinduism.

▶ Aryan Invaders

Around 1500 B.C., Aryan tribes from central Asia began sweeping over the Himalayas into India. By this time, the Indus Valley civilization had crumbled. The Aryans spread through northern India across the Gangetic Plain. They pushed many of the Indus Valley people, called Dravidians, south.

The four Vedas, collections of beliefs, prayers, and hymns, were composed by Aryans. The Vedas are the oldest Hindu sacred texts. The Aryans also created the caste system. They divided people into four castes. In the highest caste were the Aryan priests and teachers, called Brahmans. Below the Brahmans were the Kshatriyas, the rulers and warriors. Next came the Vaisyas, the merchants and farmers. In the fourth and lowest caste were the Shudras, the servants and laborers. The Dravidians ranked

Tools   Search   Notes   Discuss   Go!

so low on the social scale that they did not even have a caste. They became the untouchables, or outcastes.

The Maurya and Gupta Empires

Aryan and non-Aryan cultures blended to create the Indo-Aryan society. The Indo-Aryans established kingdoms across northern India. In 321 B.C., one of the kingdoms gained power and began pushing into southern India. It became the Maurya Empire, the first great empire in India. At its height, this empire ruled all but the southern tip of India. But by 185 B.C., the Maurya Empire had weakened. India split into hundreds of kingdoms. Over the next few centuries, several smaller empires rose up to rule regions of the subcontinent. In A.D. 319, a king

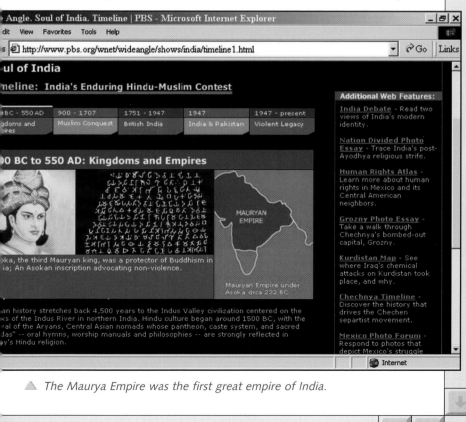

Angle. Soul of India. Timeline | PBS - Microsoft Internet Explorer

Edit   View   Favorites   Tools   Help

http://www.pbs.org/wnet/wideangle/shows/india/timeline1.html   Go   Links

ul of India

meline: India's Enduring Hindu-Muslim Contest

Additional Web Features:

| BC - 550 AD | 900 - 1707 | 1751 - 1947 | 1947 | 1947 - present |
| doms and pires | Muslim Conquest | British India | India & Pakistan | Violent Legacy |

0 BC to 550 AD: Kingdoms and Empires

MAURYAN EMPIRE

Mauryan Empire under Asoka drca 232 BC

oka, the third Mauryan king, was a protector of Buddhism in ia; An Asokan inscription advocating non-violence.

an history stretches back 4,500 years to the Indus Valley civilization centered on the ks of the Indus River in northern India. Hindu culture began around 1500 BC, with the al of the Aryans, Central Asian nomads whose pantheon, caste system, and sacred das" -- oral hymns, worship manuals and philosophies -- are strongly reflected in y's Hindu religion.

India Debate - Read two views of India's modern identity.

Nation Divided Photo Essay - Trace India's post-Ayodhya religious strife.

Human Rights Atlas - Learn more about human rights in Mexico and its Central American neighbors.

Grozny Photo Essay - Take a walk through Chechnya's bombed-out capital, Grozny.

Kurdistan Map - See where Iraq's chemical attacks on Kurdistan took place, and why.

Chechnya Timeline - Discover the history that drives the Chechen separtist movement.

Mexico Photo Forum - Respond to photos that depict Mexico's struggle

Internet

The Maurya Empire was the first great empire of India.

named Chandragupta I united northern India into the Gupta Empire. Art, music, literature, and science flourished under this empire. The Gupta rule lasted until the Huns invaded from central Asia in 550. India was again ruled by a series of smaller kingdoms.

In the eleventh century, Muslims began raiding northwestern India. They came from what is now Afghanistan. Within two hundred years, they had conquered northern India.

The Mughal Empire

In 1526, Mongols invaded India from central Asia. They created the Mughal Empire, which spread throughout most of India. The Mughals were also Muslims. They had a passion for art and literature. They built imposing forts, magnificent palaces, and other grand structures, including the Taj Mahal. Mughal rulers were usually tolerant of other religions, including Hinduism, Buddhism, Zoroastrianism, and Christianity. Akbar, one of the greatest Mughal emperors, brought both Muslims and Hindus together in his government.

The Raj

In the 1500s, European countries began looking for cheaper ways to obtain valuable Indian spices. Portugal, Denmark, Holland, France, and England established trading companies in India. European ships sailed around Africa to ports in southern India. They brought Indian spices and fabrics back to Europe. European countries fought wars to control Indian trade.

England finally won these wars. The English East India Company was the official British trading company in India. The East India Company established factories

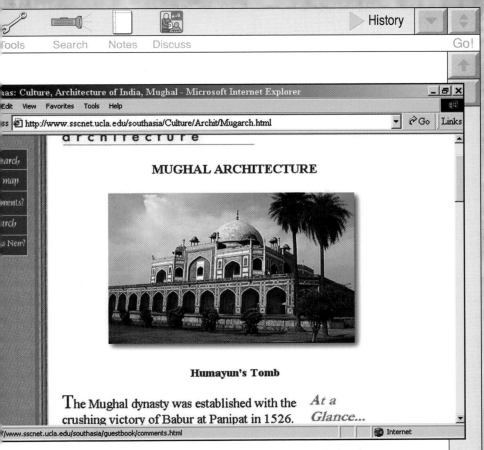

▲ *Humayun's tomb, built in 1570, is an example of Mughal architecture.*

and founded the cities of Calcutta and Madras. The Mughal Empire had crumbled, and the East India Company began taking over regions of India. By 1803, the British ruled most of the subcontinent. In 1857, after a revolt by Indian soldiers in the British army was brutally put down, England officially declared India a British colony.

The period of British rule is called the Raj. During the Raj, the British built more schools and universities, hospitals, telegraphs, irrigation canals, and roads. They constructed the Indian railway. The British attempted to modernize India, and gave some Indians high-paying jobs.

But they also imposed unfair taxes upon the citizens of India, and Indians who could not pay these taxes lost their land. The rule of the British Raj was sometimes brutal and often discriminated against the Indian people themselves.

▶ Partition and Independence

By the end of the 1800s, many Indians began pushing for their freedom. In 1885, they formed the Indian National Congress Party. This group led the fight for independence. But most members were Hindu. Muslims were afraid the Indian National Party would not represent them fairly. In 1906, they formed their own group, the All-India Muslim League.

Mohandas Karamchand Gandhi, known as Mahatma, led Indians in nonviolent resistance against the British. He called this resistance satyagraha. Under Gandhi's guidance, Indians organized peaceful marches, hunger strikes, and boycotts of British goods. The British jailed many Indians, including Gandhi. But the British soon realized they would not be able to control India much longer. They began making plans to grant India its independence, although this process would take more than thirty years.

The Muslim League pushed for a separate nation for Indian Muslims. Great Britain decided to divide India into two countries: India and Pakistan. Indians refer to this division as Partition. On August 14, 1947, Pakistan became an independent Muslim nation. The next day, August 15, 1947, India became independent.

Partition thrust India into bloody turmoil, since many Muslims still lived in India and Hindus and Sikhs lived in what was now Pakistan. Partition split some Indian states, such as the Punjab in the west and Bengal in the east, between India and Pakistan. The people living in these areas found that half their state was suddenly a foreign country. Overflowing trains began taking Muslims to Pakistan and Hindus and Sikhs to India. Over ten million people fled from one country to the other. Tension was high. In the Punjab, fighting broke out between religious groups. It is estimated that between 250,000 and 1 million people died. India and Pakistan have remained bitter enemies. In the years since independence, the two countries have fought three wars.

Soon after independence, India and Pakistan went to war over Kashmir, a region in the northernmost part of the Indian subcontinent that was home to many Muslims. To stop the fighting, the United Nations negotiated a cease-fire between the two countries. The agreement

▲ *This memorial in Madras is dedicated to Indira Gandhi, pictured, who served as India's prime minister for more than fifteen years.*

divided Kashmir at the Line of Control, which is the most widely accepted borderline of India and Pakistan. The northwestern third of Kashmir came under Pakistan's control and is called Pakistan Occupied Kashmir. The central and eastern two thirds of Kashmir remained in India.

The newly independent India was a republic. Its first prime minister was Jawaharlal Nehru, who had been president of the Indian National Congress and had worked with Gandhi to make India an independent nation. Nehru governed until his death in 1964. A skilled politician and speaker, Nehru guided India through its early difficult days as a republic. His daughter, Indira Gandhi (no relation to Mahatma Gandhi), then became prime minister. She governed from 1966 to 1977 and again from 1980 to 1984. She was assassinated by two of her bodyguards. The bodyguards were Sikhs who were outraged that she had sent soldiers into a Sikh temple. Indira Gandhi's son, Rajiv Gandhi, then became prime minister. In 1991, he was killed by terrorists from the nearby island country of Sri Lanka. His widow, Sonia Gandhi, then became active in Indian politics.

The 1990s saw India prosper economically. But it was also a decade of political turmoil inside and outside the country. India continued to have border disputes with Bangladesh and Pakistan. Inside India, tensions increased between Muslims and Hindus. In 1998, India set off underground nuclear explosions, which led the United States to impose economic sanctions against India. Pakistan also began nuclear tests, and the tense situation between the two countries led to a fear in 2002 that a nuclear war might be waged by these neighboring powers. But nuclear war was averted, and by May 2003, India and Pakistan had resumed diplomatic relations.

Chapter 6

Indian Americans

In 1790, a man from Madras, India, visited the state of Massachusetts. It was the first time a person from India had ventured to the United States. In the two centuries since that time, Indian Americans have become one of the most successful immigrant groups in the country.

▶ Coming to America

During the nineteenth century, a few people from India trickled into America. These immigrants were usually indentured servants or sailors on merchant ships.

In the 1890s, more Indians began coming to the United States, and most of these were from the Punjab, a state in northwestern India. Many had lost their farms in India because of the harsh taxes they had to pay to the British government. They came to the United States to find better jobs. Many Indian immigrants settled in Washington, Oregon, and northern California. They took jobs working on railroads, lumber mills, and farms.

As with many immigrant groups, Indians were not always welcomed by American workers, who feared that Indians, willing to work for low wages, would steal their jobs. There was also a mistrust of Indians, whose religion, dress, and food were so much different from their own. The United States already had a law that banned Chinese immigration. In 1917, the government passed another law that prevented Indians and other Asians from entering the country. Indians could not own land in the United States nor could they become American citizens.

After World War II, the United States changed its immigration laws. The government began permitting one hundred Indians to enter the country each year. Indians could also own land and become citizens. In 1965, the government again reformed its law. The new law allowed twenty thousand Indians to enter the United States each year. The law gave preference to immigrants who had relatives living in the United States or who had job skills needed in the United States. Many highly trained professionals, including doctors and computer engineers, began emigrating from India.

▶ Indian-American Life

Today about 1.6 million Indian Americans live in the United States.[1] Indians are one of the fastest growing immigrant groups in the nation. Indian Americans are also one of the wealthiest and most highly educated groups in the country. The average income of Indian-American families is higher than the average income of all Americans. A higher number of Indian Americans graduate from high school and college than the national average.[2]

Indians come to the United States to work in fields such as medicine, science, computers, technology, and university education. Many Indian Americans have started their own businesses, such as technology firms or hotels. While Indian Americans live in every state in the United States, the largest Indian-American populations are in California, Texas, New York, New Jersey, and Illinois.

Some Indian Americans have had to struggle against prejudice and discrimination, especially since the September 11, 2001, terrorist attacks on the World Trade Center in

▲ *Anil Srivatsa, an Indian American, broadcasts an English-language radio program from his home in North Brunswick, New Jersey. His program addresses the concerns of Indian Americans in the United States.*

New York and the Pentagon in Arlington, Virginia. Unfortunately, some Americans attacked other Americans they thought were Arabs or Muslims. Some Indian Americans, particularly Sikhs wearing turbans, became victims of this violence.

▷ Famous Indian Americans

Indian Americans have made a lasting impact on many areas of American life, including science, technology, business, medicine, and the arts.

Deepak Chopra is a doctor and popular author. He was born in New Delhi, the capital of India. He came to the United States in 1970 to practice medicine. Dr. Chopra has woven eastern ideas of meditation, philosophy, and religion into western medicine and health. His books have become best-sellers worldwide.

India has a thriving movie industry, and many Indian Americans have become successful in American films. Deepak Chopra's son, Gotham Chopra, is a reporter for Channel One, the news program broadcast to schools across the country. He is also the story editor for the comic-book series *Bulletproof Monk,* which became a movie in 2003.

M. Night Shyamalan is one of the most successful screenwriters and directors in Hollywood. He was born in India and grew up in Philadelphia, Pennsylvania. Shyamalan's movies include *The Sixth Sense* and *Signs.*

Ismail Merchant is a film producer and director. He was born in Bombay, India, and moved to the United States to study for his master's degree. Merchant's movies with coproducer and director James Ivory include the award-winning *A Room With a View, Howards End, Mr. and Mrs. Bridge,* and *Remains of the Day.*

Mira Nair writes, directs, and produces films. Her movies include *Mississippi Masala, The Perez Family,* and *Monsoon Wedding.* Nair was born in Bhubaneshwar, India. She moved to the United States in 1976 upon winning a scholarship to Harvard University.

Music is an important part of Indian culture, and many Indian Americans have become music stars in the United States. Norah Jones is a popular singer and musician. Her first album won eight Grammy awards in 2003. Jones is the daughter of Ravi Shankar, an Indian sitar

Conductor Zubin Mehta and his wife, Nancy, light a traditional Indian lamp at a ceremony inaugurating his father's music foundation in Bombay.

musician who became well-known in the 1960s for his association with the Beatles. Shankar popularized Indian music in western countries.

Zubin Mehta is a world-renowned classical music conductor. He was born in Bombay, India. His father founded the Bombay Symphony. In 1962, Mehta became music director of the Los Angeles Philharmonic. He was twenty-five years old—the youngest person ever to conduct an American orchestra. He served in that position from 1962 to 1978, and then served as music director of the New York Philharmonic Orchestra from 1978 to 1991.

India's first prime minister, Jawaharlal Nehru, knew that India would need scientists and engineers if India was to be able to compete internationally. To train these scientists and engineers, he founded the Indian Institute of Technology.[3] Science education has been important in India ever since, and many Indian scientists have moved to the United States. Kalpana Chawla was an astronaut and the first Indian American to fly aboard a space shuttle. She was born in Karnal, India. She came to the United States

▲ Indian Americans have distinguished themselves in many fields, including science. Subramanyan Chandrasekhar, known as Chandra, was a Nobel Prize-winning scientist in physics, and a NASA observatory now bears his name.

in 1982 to study for her master's and doctoral degrees. She completed her first space mission in 1997. Unfortunately, on February 1, 2003, Dr. Kalpana Chawla and six other astronauts died when their space shuttle, the *Columbia*, broke apart while reentering Earth's atmosphere.

Several Indian-American scientists have won Nobel Prizes. Har Gobind Khorana was one of the winners of the Nobel Prize in Medicine or Physiology in 1968. He and two other American scientists received the prize for their work in gene research. In 1983, Subramanyan Chandrasekhar won the Nobel Prize in Physics for his research on the structure of stars. He was known as Chandra, and in 1998, NASA named the Chandra X-ray Observatory after him.

Other Indian-American scientists include Narinder Kapany, who discovered fiber optics, and Vinod Dham, the senior designer of Intel's Pentium microchip. Amar Bose designed the Bose speaker system, which created more lifelike sound than previous stereo speakers. Bose was born in the United States. His parents emigrated from Calcutta, India.

Indian Americans have also become successful entrepreneurs and business people. Vinod Khosla cofounded Sun Microsystems. Sabeer Bhatia founded Hotmail. Indian-American journalist Snigdha Prakash reports on business and the economy for National Public Radio. In 1999 she won the South Asian Journalists Association's Journalism Award.

Indian Americans have overcome obstacles and discrimination to make good lives for themselves in this country. In doing so, they have also contributed a great deal to their new country while retaining the culture and heritage of their homeland.

India Facts

1. "India," *The World Factbook 2003,* n.d., <http://www.cia.gov/cia/publications/factbook/geos/in.html> (October 15, 2003).

2. Ibid.

Chapter 2. Land and Climate

1. "World-Wide Rainfall Extremes Chart," National Weather Service Hydrometeorological Design Studies Center, n.d., <http://www.nws.noaa.gov/oh/hdsc/max_precip/maxprecip.htm> (May 14, 2003).

2. Antonia Cunningham, ed., *Guinness World Records 2002* (London: Guinness World Records Ltd., 2002), p. 85.

Chapter 3. Culture

1. "India," *The World Factbook 2003,* n.d., <http://www.cia.gov/cia/publications/factbook/geos/in.html> (March 19, 2003).

Chapter 4. Economy

1. Lesley Stahl, "Imported From India," *60 Minutes,* CBS News, transcript of March 2, 2003, episode.

2. "Introduction to Bollywood Cinema," Turner Classic Movies, 2003, n.d., <http://www.turnerclassicmovies.com/ThisMonth/Article/0,,27939,00,html> (October 19, 2003).

Chapter 6. Indian Americans

1. Jessica S. Barnes and Claudette E. Bennett, *The Asian Population: 2000,* U.S. Department of Commerce, U.S. Census Bureau, Washington, D.C., February 2002, p. 8.

2. *We, the Americans: Asians,* U.S. Department of Commerce, Bureau of the Census, Washington, D.C., September 1993, pp. 4, 6, and 7.

3. Lesley Stahl, "Imported From India," *60 Minutes,* CBS News, transcript of March 2, 2003, episode.

Further Reading

Bradnock, Robert, and Roma Bradnock. *India Handbook*. Bath, England: Footprint Books Limited, 1998.

Bryan, Nichol. *Indian Americans*. Edina, Minn.: ABDO Publishing Co., 2003.

Cervera, Isabel. *The Mughal Empire*. Chicago: Children's Press, 1994.

Cruz, Barbara C. *Multiethnic Teens and Cultural Identity*. Berkeley Heights, N.J.: Enslow Publishers, Inc., 2001.

Cumming, David. *India*. Austin, Tex.: Raintree Steck-Vaughn, 2002.

Ganeri, Anita. *India*. London, UK: Belitha Press, 2003.

Gordon, Susan. *Asian Indians*. New York: Franklin Watts, 1990.

Kalman, Bobbie. *India: The Land*. New York: Crabtree Publishing Co., 2001.

Lamba, Abha Narain. *India*. New York: DK Publishing, 2002.

Middleton, Haydn. *Mother Teresa*. Chicago: Heinemann Library, 2001.

Moorcroft, Christine. *The Taj Mahal*. Austin, Tex.: Raintree Steck-Vaughn, 1998.

Nicholson, Louise. *National Geographic Traveler: India*. Washington, D.C.: National Geographic Society, 2001.

Pollard, Michael. *The Ganges*. New York: Benchmark Books, 1998.

Severance, John B. *Gandhi: Great Soul*. New York: Clarion, 1997.

Index